Counterglow

Patricia Killelea

Crossroads Poetry Series
Three Fires Confederacy
Waawiiyaatanong
Windsor, ON ✦ Detroit, MI

First Edition. February 2019

Library and Archives Canada Cataloguing in Publication

Killelea, Patricia, 1983-, author
    Counterglow / Patricia Killelea.

(Crossroads poetry series)
Poems.
ISBN 978-1-988214-24-5 (softcover)

    I. Title.

PS3611.I443C68 2018   811'.6   C2018-906431-5

Book cover design: D.A. Lockhart
Cover Image: "They run like deer, jump like deer and think like deer." by Ibayarifin, Ink/Paper 2018.
Book layout: D.A. Lockhart
Author Photo: Two Crows

Published in the United States of America and Canada by

Urban Farmhouse Press
www.urbanfarmhousepress.com

The Crossroads Poetry Series is a line of books that showcases established and emerging poetic voices from across North America. The books in this series represent what the editors at UFP believe to be some of the strongest voices in both American and Canadian poetics. Counterglow is the eighth book in this series.

Printed in Californian FB font

CONTENTS

I: *Stood in the Shine*

II: *Book of the Wound*

III: *How to Burn*

c o u n t e r g l o w: also known as gegenschein.
astronomical term for the opposition effect.
a faint brightening of the night sky in the region of the antisolar point
caused by interplanetary dust; the counterglow can only be detected
when one observes from a place devoid of light.

I: Stood in the Shine

THE ALMOST-PRAYER

Help me to remember the edge of speech:
I know it had to do with hunger and stunted hands
squeezing the last crumbs of what doesn't last.

The sound of it all: a terrible test pooling at our feet.

What to name our coming days if not the sound of furious
melting, what's heard gasping between stolen breaths on stolen lands,
our words breaking apart in sheets floating further south.

....

Help me also to return from the starving grounds:
I know there is a space from which the ancestors watch us.
I stopped there once between two trains about to collide

and I was the missing set of tracks I was the absence of wind I was the glacier melting
and drowning the last word ever questioned.

It tasted like spoiled deer-meat and everyone was afraid.

RETROGRADE

It is not morning hinting
at the curtain's red edges—

It's the meteor come to end us.
It's the light from atom bombs.

What severs has returned;
winds have come.

Winds have come
to cover your life with sand.
Your story is not allowed.

A snake lays eggs in your word.

HONEST LIGHT

We're leaden with ghosts,
	with doors that won't stay shut.

We never knew how many bodies
	would come and go,
		mostly go;

How many times we'd have to stand
	in sharpest rain,

digested without voice.

No days enter without knives;
no faces exit without trace.

Beside and among me, they
reside— the faded
ones, the former loves.

				Even honest light
				fails.

THE MARIGOLDS FOR SHIRLEY

I made a maze of half
your death, there where
the water doesn't gleam.

I made a barque of
your final voice, set out
for the center where god
measures darkness
under its breath.

All   these   numbers:

numbers I hold onto
before your shards + ashes,
amid the ruins of shrines
I built to memorize

the outline of your black hair,
altars I can't stop finding
my way
         out of.

I can't stop counting,
                    mother,
counting out
              the marigolds—

HOW TO STOP THE BLEEDING

Separate me into what's real and what's spoken,
and I'll show you the ocean sprouting up between the two.

Each morning, you arrive at the doorstep of my voice
and turn away before knocking, so no one ever answers.

I am trying to explain the doorstep and the seashells I set aside
after failing to find a song for the tidepools after Fukushima.

You remind me that shells are made of keratin, just like hair & nails
and suddenly I'm inadequate for not taking the form of a spiral.

Somewhere I am finding a rhyme scheme outside of tides and sound,
based instead on the color of a leaf about to change into autumn.

I've been searching my whole life for moments that step away
from brightness, and I'm getting closer every day.

Twice in that searching I've come across a dead bird in the sand,
and I didn't know if I should say hello or goodbye.

I keep setting my own body down inside that same question
of language, but I still don't know how to stop the bleeding.

SCAPULAR

How, as a child,
I wanted to be

staved and holy;
so donned the brown

stiff ribbons, their two
small squares of text

over my heart, atop my spine—

> *Whoever dies*
> *in this garment shall be*
> *preserved*
> *forever from hell*

read that square,
read the square I wore.

Of all assurances,

O mother,
O man,

this is the one
I can never forgive.

TRANSMISSION
for Chandra Womack

I drag tule reed through an ink
drawn from Suisun blackberries
across the belly of a tundra swan—

It's a message for you,
you stirring there

beneath the long light
of an even longer sun
       far   far north;

And when the swans return
to arctic grounds,
      you read into the juice
      still soaked in white plumage—

I have lain the crimson word.
I have lain the crimson word.

THE NARROWING

Your face came into focus
just before your final heave.

I stood in the shine, then,
of no one, the cry,

borrowed time
sealing off the sound.

       Your hands, mother, by candlelight.
       Your mystery in the room.

THE SMALL

Somewhere there are smallish hooves
approaching where waters meet reed;
perhaps even asters weave
beside the ripples, beside the hooves.

I have thoughts of creatures.
The thoughts bring me such comfort, and I begin
to love my image of all the smallish beings.

But they do not gather for me—
they gather for what life needs.
A bit of shelter, a bit of blood.

My idea of all the smallish things
is my bit of tender shame.

I will not stay here much longer.

ARS POETICA

A curtain of ruin is lifted:

I sing the trenches there,
bowing to scorched voices.

      Armies

        of

      constellations.

HIGH SIERRA

Closer to sky at this
altitude, we dethorn,

retry dreaming—
It's the pine and poplar;

not number, but sheen...
That sense of light surrounding

even us;
We who must break

bones to remember
this; Who must resist

the weight to turn away.

HOW IT STARTS

You carry a headful of numbers
from room to room, you carry
the sound of everyone counting all at once
just to play the feeling backwards
while you're sleeping.

Your numbers set alphabets on fire
whenever red rises in the comment section.

Yes, it's blood— it's always been blood.

They'll see to it that even your ghost stays angry,
that you go on picking berries with ghost hands.
How else will you stave off being overtaken?

Rooms upon rooms covered in thorns, can you imagine.

You must believe me when I say
that I could touch you & you wouldn't even notice—
I'll pass right through you, I'm so invisible from loss.

On the train, I count the number of hands
reaching & reaching for their phones; eager
for completion like a fishhook, a knife sheath, an urn.

That's just one way we've learned how to ghost.

You should know by now there's no such thing
as clickbait: only the fear of not knowing
where the blood is coming from next & the quiet
just before the stars
are torn out from under you.

If you must brush against each name of our dead
to scroll to the bottom of history, how much time
will it take for your fingers to burn down to bone?

Soon there will be no more counting.

Someday the gods
are going to put us all down for good,
and this is how it starts.

II: Book of the Wound

"Light thinks it travels faster than anything
but it is wrong. No matter how fast light travels,
it finds the darkness has always got there first,
and is waiting for it."
                                —Terry Pratchett

1493

This face is a weapon now,
ripe as stone.

This word is building
a cocoon.

A mouth (but whose?)
circles darkness—

AN GORTA MÓR

There is not enough sky to heal you.

Again: you have no between, no cracks.
You are the solid despair.

Go to your land (it is not your land)
and dry out. Uproot your face.

Do not return for anyone—
the keening in you accumulates.

THE KNELL

Summer goes then, the knife
in the eye, a word past skin.

Hovels have been made
of the home in you,

      and across two mountains
      a procession has been moving

toward you, toward you alone.

You double-check the latches,
tend to all your ruins,

yet what's approaching
still arrives: and with it

the bright pain chimes.

LITTLE HOUR CANTICLE

Here the hour awakens the dead at my throat.
Here also the char and the charred brush.
Here the genuflections I kept at bay,
& here the new law which brings the thorn.

Now I can lie down with lions—
Now I can plant a word that gives off shade—
Now the world is all at home without the gods,
even as I'm avalanched by grace.

Here and now, the hour
answers to its endless names:

You who can't remain, you who can't remain.

MAPPING THE MOTHLIGHT

I knew you by the way you came to me with knives,
eyes lowered from a life spent crouching in the bonefield.

But you've carried, too, the voices of animals, so I stop
to listen: I can hear you scattering their cries like breadcrumbs,
a path to find your way back to a world that isn't burning.

Tonight we will gather up all of our history and roll it out like dough.
Once all of our stories are flattened, the dust will settle around your tongue,
making it impossible to explain the stillness at the center of a flake of snow.

Tell me where my mouth is because my body can't remember.
I must have left it down past the creek where the wilderness moves
across the gray stones, where we walked from one sun to the next.

I've dressed up all of my words like an altar in the season of dying,
and now if I were to name the darkness, I would run out of voice.

Whenever I sleep beside you, I dream of moths giving their wings
away to the flame; tell me is it normal to believe in prophecy & the ghost of it all,

is it worth it to rise each morning to count the pine needles and the blame.
Tell me if I am the wing or if I am the fire and why I should ever believe you.

DIVIDING THE FLOCK

The sound of hunger
splintering bone again,

a single gunshot
dividing the flock.

> There is a great sorting
> among beings—

> the stillness
> which follows

is another lie.

NIGHT ON KLAMATH RIVER

Sleeping awkward on its mangled stones,
the river told me to dream of two fawns.

> One leapt into me and bedded from there.
> The other was shy, nuzzling shadows.

> They were gangrenous, infested.
> Open sores shining out from their sockets...

Come morning, I turned my back to that river
and all its feverish rapids, but now

something in me lies down
at the thought of hurried does

calling out to their young,
rustling just outside my field of vision.

> *My heart: you were thinnest there,*
> *where the sick ghosts of fawns*
> *followed you home from the other world.*

I HAVE KEPT A LIGHT ON FOR YOU

I have kept a light on for you:
a taste in the air around you,

something for your seething.

      I feel the way this makes me
      smaller too;   how the whole body

      can burn away

in the name of not letting go.

THE HUNGRIEST ANIMAL ALIVE

What do you see   when you look through the bullet hole
in a crow's wing?   *sky sky* or a window to surviving humankind,
how to disappear into cloud instead of learning how to die—

Between the black and the blue   bleeds a new kind of light,
an answer to the question of who has what right to take   & keep taking &
the hollows take a lifetime to memorize   but I cannot look aside.

We're living in a starving land that wants to learn to fly,
but what's the use of feathers if we cannot trust the sky? Let me tell you:
fear is still the hungriest animal alive   & who is more afraid than man?

I'm taking to clouds and finding windows where I can,
but that still doesn't mean   what you think it means.
When I look through a bullet hole in a crow's wing
                                        I see everything.

NO RECOLLECTIONS IN TRANQUILITY

The word which fell
from the nest—

You've lifted it up,
back into air

      but your mouth
      won't recognize it
      as its own.

      The scent
      of the word
      has changed.

You cease
incubating

the wound—
      You build now
      into your tongue

      the newly-woven
      opacities,

      evasive
      brightness,

shrine for the utterance
barred from returning.

HANDFUL OF CROWS

We have heaved across red
crags, tucked the dead roots
long inside—

My ones: where might we rest,

rest from the shadows
we carry?

THE FIELD

Something said there trampled
bones to dust, said there
in the place of sheaves.

Something said there circled
each brightness we found and found
each brightness to be a lie.

And something was said and stacked
against furrows, was said and shriveled
the roots unmasked before us.

> We are nearing that field once again,
> only this time
> we will outlast the night.

> We are nearing the place
> where words are finally

> enough.

MIGRATIONS

Some fleck of your darkness
    fell away there

and you crept up closer
to be among the living—

sounded out *arise*
for the very first time

— as if you'd only just arrived
           in this world,

stepped recently into dislodged stone
and the mountain (sounding you out)

still remembered your shape.

POSTCARDS FROM THE DEAD

How far you've carried the chasm—
for all your human days.

(You say, too, you've crawled the stones,
found no shelter in the moss)

Did I not feed you?
Did I not bathe you in the reeds?

III: How to Burn

GEGENSCHEIN

I've gone now to the shadow-passages,
     through that hushed land.

When I found you there, too,
     I wept, I wept.

Who knows, besides, what we speak of?
     Above us, the dragonflies,

newfound in blue,
     hover among our decibels.

This whispering you and I do...
     it exposes a nest.

I cup my brown hands toward you.
     Within: two smoothed eggs,

unburdening, growing
     less overcast.

These are the true hearts
     plucked from the lasting.

We measure out the shrines,
     we nurse ourselves clean.

We pray with one voice
     in the counterglow.

IF THIS WORD STAYS WHOLE

You are the sea again— vast
& malleable, beings dying inside you.

I count off all the parts you gave away:
tooth of your worry,
fin of what you couldn't find,
claws which wouldn't fend.

Is it true—

do we speak only
at the shores
of one another,
voices hacking against immeasurable deeps?

This word foams, then.
This word is high tide come to renew.
This word is hatching in the moonlight,
making its way through granules

to you,

And if this word stays whole: all of your parts will be restored.

ABOUT HISTORY

Come dark, I pluck visions from between your teeth
because there's not enough dream to go around.

I count syllables all night on the ceiling instead—
little particles of sound rising from the tips of your lashes.

I take you into my lungs, thinking you'll sedate me,
but it only makes me wild again, & I leap from the bed

on four legs while you go on sleeping.
Under skin, there is surely muscle and bone

but beneath your resting face there's something furious,
bright as moonlight kept behind sealed glass.

My tides are boiling now because your glow is so near,
and all the ancient beings inside of me float to the surface.

Our bodies are mostly water our bodies are memory
and from this body, I learn by heart the rise & fall

of your chest until sunrise, and that is all I need to know

about history.

DISTANT RELATIVES (APHORISMS)

Every lie you'll ever swallow will have something to do with forever.

*

The best animals know how to stay hidden. Deep down, everyone knows this.

*

Some feelings must be set to music and exorcised.

*

You come across a language that injects eggs into the reader.

*

Each word is a black hole. Each star: a mouth chewing loudly.

*

The best way to ensure aloneness is to write your name
on a piece of paper + then set that paper on fire.

*

Because you are 60% water, it is best to speak of the ocean
as if she is listening.

*

Still, it is not language that unlocks the waters.

MOTHER TONGUE

Words are anglers.
That's what was said.
We bite, we're dragged
across seabottom—

unkicking at first,
charmed.

> I hear you listening in,
> traveled-through. Recall:
> we come from the gilled.
> Speech needs us.

> ....

In a cave on mute
cliff, you tried
drinking the low tide.

No, I am not the one
who can trace
moans in the sand.

> ....

It's a beach, love— we're here
to feel small, to take in
what doesn't need us.

Put a shell

> *to your ear and hear*
> *a shell.*

AXIS

It doesn't wince much to measure the dead—
only what this living leaves behind:
the trails of muck & wine, the throes
between the beaten wing & beaten eye.

It stings far more to weigh what shines—
the pale reach of mapping hands,
the sound of sky assessed & scored.

> *Mama I mean to measure you by suns*
> *Mama I mean to not measure someday*

WHEN I FAIL TO GLOW

When I fail to glow,
I come to the book;

to the ash-bright
pain tangled into your word.

What would you have me do?

I walk through the yard
sifting for your face

in the wet-dark leaves,
your voice in the owl screech.

I turn over heavy stones
listening for your lungs.

Some nights, I even find you there:
pressed beneath the hard-damp loam,

down

where the
syllables
waken

and
gleam—

RADIANCE

In a meteor swarm,
the only sin is blinking

yet I close my lids
the second I sight
the slightest stirring,

this way my ears
are showered with
the awe of others.

I allow myself this nearness,
have learned to only open

my eyes once all returns
to silence.
This is the way

I show myself
that sorrow comes first,
then god.

NEW SCRIPTURES

I try to enter an æon:
the one at the center of my skull,

but something needs a bridge there—
a way to cross the river that drinks from me.

When I listen too closely, I'm blinded
by the sound,
                so many speaking all at once.

Shapes made of our watching
circle near us, and through—

We are moving around in the word,
into the light above the stone.

        (There is a voice that can be seen
        There is a voice that also sees)

OMPHALOS

In a farther hour: consensus.
The world must be hacked up anew.

You and I: cloudy, unfamiliar again;
not as two from usual soil,

but out of the way, to be reached for.

No one then   unearths us,   none,

for we have prepared
an altar of centers,

made music from hunger,

      returned to the secret
      original burrow—

CULMINATIONS

Something has passed
from one mouth to the next—

not a taste, but a tome

delivered,
                  held   aloft.

A great gray light
hesitates   inside.

              Here on the inland sea,
              all the colors are aged,

but a face, but a face
finally stirs

HOW TO BURN

Come to the place of names— trust
that it is a real place.

Draw now the curtains low
& lie down beside yourself alone

without mirrors, without sheets.

Outside, blackbirds pepper the sky
and that is a real place too.

>　*Remember high desert*
>　*your blood once called home—*
>
>　*Remember the blackness*
>　*where lightning taught*
>　*juniper how to burn—*

By inner compass:　　　come
to the names circling before you,

and in that circling
come to know
how your name, too,
belongs among them,

>　*has always*
>　*belonged among them.*

Between　　　　the air

　　　　　　　　　& the blackbirds
　　　　listen:

WORM PSALM

I spent a year

down
       in the red
clay—

       That's how I learned
       there are no

clean

       mysteries

NOTES

Gegenschein and **Radiance**: originally in *Spiritus*

No Recollections in Tranquility: title refers to William Wordsworth's Preface to *Lyrical Ballads*, in which he defines poetry as, "the spontaneous overflow of powerful feelings: it takes its origin from emotion recollected in tranquility."

Honest Light: originally in *Quarterly West*

The Almost-Prayer: originally in print in *As/Us*; video poem feature at *Atticus Review*

The Narrowing: originally in "The Seizure State" at *Gigantic*

1493: originally in *cream city review*

Omphalos: from the Greek word for the center of the world, the "earth's navel." Huge stones were used to mark sites believed to be world centers, the most famous of which being the omphalos at the oracle in Delphi.

The Small: originally in *Suisun Valley Review*

The Field and **Scapular**: originally in *The Gap-Toothed Madness*

Night on Klamath River: originally in *The Common*

Worm Psalm and **New Scriptures**: originally in *Waxwing*

How to Stop the Bleeding and **Mapping the Mothlight**: originally in *Barzakh*

How it Starts: originally a video poem feature at *Poetry Film Live*

ACKNOWLEDGEMENTS

Appreciation goes to the editors of journals where poems in Counter-glow originally appeared: *Quarterly West, Waxwing, Barzakh, As/Us, The Common, Atticus Review, cream city review, Moving Poems, Spiritus, Gigantic Magazine, Poetry Film Live, Gap-Toothed Madness*, and *Suisun Valley Review*.

Thanks to the Santa Fe Art Institute for a residency that made the completion of this project possible, and to Urban Farmhouse Press for believing in this collection. Additional thanks goes to the Department of English and the Center for Native American Studies at Northern Michigan University.

I am ever grateful for the support of my family, mentors, and friends, especially: Margarite Alves, Joe Wenderoth, Inés Hernández-Avila, Sandra McPherson, April Lindala, Monica McFawn, Two Crows Siewertsen, Michael Harris, Christine Ami, Angel Hinzo, Aubrey Hess, Martha Stromberger, Kazim Ali, Pam Uschuk, Michael Wasson, Mark Burrows, Dave Bonta at Moving Poems and the whole crew at *Passages North*.

This book is dedicated to the memory of my mother, Shirley Osejo. Thank you for everything you taught me.

ABOUT THE AUTHOR

Patricia Killelea (Xicana/Irish American) is the author of *Other Suns* (Swan Scythe Press, 2011). Originally from the Bay Area, California, she is currently an Assistant Professor of English at Northern Michigan University. She holds a Ph.D. in Native American Studies (2015) and an M.A. in Creative Writing (2008) from the University of California, Davis.

She is also a digital media artist, and her poetry films have been featured in *Atticus Review,* as well as *Poetry Film Live* and *Moving Poems.* Her work has been short-listed and screened for the Ó Bhéal International Poetry Film Festival (2017), and long-listed for Rabbit Heart Poetry Film Festival (2016).

She is currently poetry editor for the literary journal *Passages North.*

CPSIA information can be obtained
at www.ICGtesting.com
Printed in the USA
FFHW020738111019
55481672-61277FF